The "First Lady c
In Her Own Woras

By Valentina Tereshkova

A SpaceHistory101.com Publication

Reprinted with the permission of the journal: "Quest: The History of Spaceflight Quarterly" http:// www.spacehistory101.com

Images courtesy of the Russian Cultural Centre, the Embassy of Russia, and NASA.

Printed in the United States of America
ISBN: 978-188702299-6

Table of Contents

Preface

Affectionately known as the "First Lady of Space," Valentina Vladimirovna "Valya" Tereshkova became the first woman to fly into space, spending nearly three days piloting *Vostok 6* beginning on 16 June 1963—twenty years before Sally Ride became the first American woman to reach orbit.

Born on 6 March 1937 in the village of Maslennikovo, Yaroslavl Oblast, in central Russia about 170 miles northeast of Moscow, Tereshkova was a textile factory assembly worker who became interested in parachuting at a young age. Hiding it from her family, she trained as a competitive skydiver at the local Aeroclub; making her first jump on 21 May 1959.

After the 1961 flight of Yuri Gagarin, Sergei Korolev, the chief Soviet rocket engineer, decided that the USSR should send a woman into space. Out of more than four hundred applicants, five were selected on 16 February 1962: Tatyana Kuznetsova, Irina Solovyova, Zhanna Yorkina, Valentina Ponomaryova, and Tereshkova. Qualifications included that they be parachutists less than 30 years of age, under 170 cm (5 feet 7 inches) tall, and under 70 kg (154 lbs.) in weight.

The group spent several months in intensive training, including rocket theory, spacecraft engineering, weightless flights, isolation tests, centrifuge tests, parachute jumps and pilot training in jet fighters. Concluding with examinations in November 1962, the remaining candidates were commissioned Junior Lieutenants in the Soviet Air Force. Tereshkova, Solovyova and Ponomaryova were the leading candidates and a joint mission profile was developed that would see a woman launched into space on a solo Vostok flight in March or April 1963.

After watching the successful launch of Valery Bykovsky in *Vostok 5* on 14 June 1963, Tereshkova began final preparations for her own flight. She was 26 at the time. On the morning of 16 June 1963, Tereshkova and her back-up Solovyova were both dressed in spacesuits and taken to the launch pad by bus. After completing her communication and life support checks, she was sealed inside the Vostok. After a two-hour countdown, *Vostok 6* launched faultlessly, and Tereshkova became the first woman in space. Her call sign in this flight was Chaika [Seagull].

Tereshkova spent nearly three days in space, orbiting the Earth 48 times. On this flight, she logged more flight time than the combined time of all American astronauts who had flown before that date. Tereshkova maintained a flight log and took photographs of the horizon, which were later used to identify aerosol layers within the atmosphere.

Several months after the *Vostok 6* flight she married Andriyan Nikolayev (1929–2004) on 3 November 1963 at the Moscow Wedding Palace. Khrushchev presided at the wedding party attended by top government and space program leaders.

On 8 June 1964, she gave birth to a daughter, Elena Andrianovna Nikolaeva-Tereshkova, who grew up to become a doctor; and the first person to have both a mother and father who traveled into space.

Valentina and Nikolayev divorced in 1982. She later remarried orthopedist Yuliy Shaposhnikov, who passed away in 1999.

Following her career as a cosmonaut, she became a prominent member of the Communist Party of the Soviet Union holding various political offices including head of the Russian Cultural Centers around the globe. It was while in this position she contributed some of her memoirs to the history journal, *Quest: The History of Spaceflight*, the first time any had been published in English.

* * *

Valentina Vladimirovna Tereshkova

Born: **6 March 1937**
Birth City: **Maslennikovo**
Birth State: **Yaroslavl**
Birth Country: **Russia**

Personal
Married, 1963 to Andriyan Nikolayev, a fellow Cosmonaut.
Divorced in 1980.

Daughter: Elena Andrianovna
Father: Vladimir Tereshkova, a tractor driver; killed in action during
        World War II.
Mother: Elena Fedorovna, worked in a textile plant.
Siblings: Younger brother (Vladimir), older sister (Ludmilla)

Astronaut Career
Date Selected for Astronaut Program: 12 March 1962
Group: 1962 Femal Group Detachment, TsPK-Fc
Departed from Soviet Space Program: 1969
Launch Date: *Vostok 6*, 16 June 1963
Call Sign: Chaika (Seagull)
Flight Time: 2.95 days

Flight Overview
Vostok 6, joint flight with *Vostok 5*. First woman in space and the only woman to go into space until Svetlana Savitskaya, 19 years later. On its first orbit, *Vostok 6* came within about five km of *Vostok 5*, the closest distance achieved during the flight and established radio contact. Recovered 1963 8:20 GMT, Landed 53:16 N 80:27 E

Career Highlights
- 162 parachute jumps.
- Russian Air Force Major General
- Ph.D. in Engineering
- Elected to Russian legislature
- Popular speaker around the globe including the United Nations
- Named "Woman of the Century" in London, October 2000, by International Women of the Year Association
- Has a crater on the Moon named after her.
- Order of Lenin.
- Honored as Hero of the Soviet Union
- United Nations Gold Medal of Peace
- Joliet-Curie Gold Medal

The First Lady of Space Remembers
By Valentina Tereshkova

PEOPLE AND STARS

When a warm clear night falls and our town (Yaroslavl) is plunged into sleep, I like to sit at the window and look out at the starry sky. Occasionally the wind will whisper something from the tops of the tall pine and then everything again silent. In such minutes I remember the most bright and wonder my life: the flight into space.

I know that our small town is called "Star City" because cosmonauts, my "heavenly brothers," live there. Some of their names are already known all over the world and there are others who have yet to discover their ways in the universe for the achievement of the human mind and the glory of the Motherland.

But sometimes I think that the town received its name because the stars above it appear especially bright, clear, as if washed; and so close that one could reach out ones hand and clutch them in their palm. Maybe, that's because now I watch them with different eyes, remembering my journey into the universe. Maybe that's it... As soon as I begin staring into the starry ways in the sky, I physically realize how close they are.

Those who have already been in space, yearn with all their heart and soul to hasten there again and again.

With every single day passing, time leaves my flight in the past. New events, unforgettable impressions of meeting new people, and distant itineraries are plaited together into an ingenious ornament. Thousands of letters, handshakes, flowers and smiles...and the memory still treasures all the tiny details of everything related to my space flight. These have become my whole life.

I had a childhood dream, maybe a little brave, a little unusual, but entirely real and very possible to achieve. I always wanted to see the world with all its beauty, to learn its past and future, to guess the future, and to pass to others everything I found out and saw.

Could I have ever thought that soon enough I'll see my country and our Earth through the window of a space ship?

THE SKY IS SO CLOSE

The reason why I began attending the parachute club was my friend Galina Shashkova. We went to the college together. She was a parachute jumper and strongly recommended that her coursemates, including me, enter the aeroclub. But like many other girls, I didn't believe in my abilities very much—it looked like this sport required courage and was created for people with great will power and strong muscles. I liked sports; I could ski and swim. I swam across the Volga [river] many times, but there was nothing heroic in it.

Still once, because of mere curiosity, I went to the airport and watched some jumps. Everything seemed unusual here at first. The view of tiny little helpless figures separated from the plane made me strong in my decision; this parachute sport is not for me.

I don't remember exactly how much time passed, but I believe it was soon after this that my attention was attracted by a small ad at the Weaving Factory Number 2. The young men and women were invited to enter the shooting, radio, and motor-boating clubs. But most of all I was interested in the line "...parachute club." Then for the second time I was at the airport, got acquainted with the girls there, and noticed that they were typical girls, nice and all different, having nothing that would distinguish them from my friends and me. Moreover, some of them took off their "armor," helmets, overalls, and heavy boots, and transformed into young and fragile human beings.

I started to enjoy reading books about the pilots. I admired the courage of those who were conquering altitude and speed limits and who heroically fought in the sky for our Motherland during the war with fascists. I especially liked the memoirs of Three-Time Hero of the Soviet Union, I.N. Kozhedoub, and his stories about the women pilots of Gvardejsky Tamansky air force division, and memories about Valery Pavlovich Chkalov.

Once I saw the picture of a girl with dark eyes in a magazine. Everything about her look was attractive: her open face, her overalls, and even her name, Nadezhda Pryakhina. And then when I read that she jumped from the plane and stayed more than a minute without opening the parachute, I was shocked. Not everyone could jump and fall into a cold night for more than a minute! Could I jump with a parachute? The thought flashed across my mind. And then I started to dream about my first jump. It still seemed to me as something unreal. These days, after my more than a hundred jumps, these fears seem naive.

Once in the fall (it happened in 1958) Viktor Havronin, the skydiving instructor, gathered us and told us about the sport of parachuting. We listened with great attention. Then I became enthusiastic to try it myself, and thus I found myself near the door of the aerospace club, at Svoboda Street 9. For a long time I hesitated to go inside, looking at the pictures of parachutists and pilots and reading again the advertisement inviting the new members. Finally, I made up my mind and opened the door.

I came home later than usual. Perhaps there was something unusual in my appearance, because mom asked, "Has anything happened? You are so strange today, Valyusha." To tell her that I joined the parachute club was too hard for me. I didn't want to trouble her; besides, I was not completely sure about the success of my new adventure. Some girls from the factory attended this club before, but in a short time would quit this hobby and drop the lessons, and some girls were just not accepted because they failed the health test.

Our group started the lessons immediately. We studied the parachute, learned to put it together, were introduced to the theory of jumping, and went to the airport to watch the "veterans" jump. At the very beginning, maybe like all newcomers, I was not confident and envied experienced sportsmen who looked so confident both at the airport and in class. Preparing for the jumps, they quickly put the tents on the grass, took parachutes out of the bags, and skillfully checked them. Nobody seemed to pay attention to us, though the instructor was always near, explaining and telling us what to do.

And so it happened that finally, not yet having jumped once, we started to believe that we could be parachutists. Viktor Havronin was the person who persuaded us. He could find an excellent approach for every beginner; he was able to calm us down and provide us with the confidence we needed. And how excited he was telling us about his favorite sport! We could listen for hours.

Which jump did I remember best of all? When people ask this question, they know the answer beforehand: of course, the first one. It will remain in my memory through all my life. It was May 21, 1959. We came to the airport early in the morning. The morning was gray with a little rain. Cold wind blew the low clouds and the fog through the tops of the trees. Pools of water sparkled near the parked planes.

We became sad. Could it be that because of the weather we won't be able to jump? We were waiting for this day for so long, with so much preparation and worrying! And the bad weather destroyed everything. Our instructor checked the weather forecast a few times and said briefly, "Let's wait."

And so we waited, and finally the clouds slowly started to move away. Blue sky appeared through the clouds, and the Sun began to play on the ground. The sparrows became louder, and we were happy. We will jump today!

The small YaK [airplane] started to roll, jumping on the little bumps, and smoothly separated from the ground. Then it reached the proper height. Here is the sky! It's so close. I listened carefully, being afraid that I would miss the signal "Go!" in the loud roar of the motor. Maybe because I lost the sense of time, maybe I was nervous, as it always happens when you're expecting something big and important to happen in your life, I suddenly believed that it was time for me to jump.

Something tore apart inside of me, and with eyes closed, I made a step into nowhere. A few seconds of fast falling. It's hard to tell what I experienced during these short seconds. A dynamic stroke brought me back to reality and I saw a white dome over my head. Around me in the boundless blue sky flew shapeless hats of the clouds. The Volga flashed in the rays of the golden circle of the Sun. A green stripe of woods was flowing into the sky at the horizon. My heart filled with joy. The first jump! This was my first jump! I tried to pull the ropes, and the parachute started to turn. The ground was approaching.

When I felt the push with my feet, I fell on my side and the parachute stretched near me. I hardly had time to realize that everything was over, when the strict voice asked me, "Why did you jump without a command?"

I was embarrassed. Blushing, tried to explain how it all happened. According to my words, the noise of the motor, not I, was guilty. It was funny, and everybody who was listening turned away to hide smiles. I was upset with myself. But what could I do? It was clear to me that many disappointments and happy moments, successes and failures were yet to come.

And then the voice said again, "Well, ok, it was not bad for a beginner. You will learn from your mistakes. All of you have a chance to soon become good parachutists."

It was late at night when I came home. Volodya, my younger brother, met me scolding, "Where have you been? Mom was all worried about you, and she went looking for you. We'll see what she does to you!"

Mom and my sister came back at the moment when I was telling my brother why I was so late. I had to withstand a strong attack. But I was so insistent defending my new hobby, that mom, who at the very beginning kept telling me that this sport was not for women, became more and more quiet, and then finally gave up! "Valyusha," she said, "Do as you like. But please be careful. I doubt that parachute is very reliable. At least, don't jump from too high. It's really scary!"

It's air! How strongly it attracts someone who at least once felt its strong currents, leaned on them and experienced the joy of a free fall in the fifth ocean. It's not by chance that Nesterov, a famous Russian pilot, wrote that in the air there is support everywhere. If a ski jumper, when jumping, feels like a bird, then how strong should be the feeling of a sky-diver during the moments of the flight in the air, when he or she is controlling the body, rushing fearlessly toward the ground. At any time you could stop this magic flight and change the rapid falling with the whistle in the ears to a smooth descent.

The domes of the parachute! Like the balls of smoke, they flashed in the sky and tended to the ground. The feeling of victory over the height was carried from the airport by each of us. Happy and excited I returned home from the airport. There was a big and wonderful world opening for me.

Fear... Did I have it when I jumped for the first time? Yes and no. I jumped myself; nobody pushed me. And at the same time, any feelings after the first jump were very peculiar; these feelings made me close my eyes. I closed my eyes during the second jump, too, when I left the plane. During the fifth and the sixth times I could keep my eyes open, overcoming the fear.

Why does a skydiver worry so much at first? It's because everything is concentrated inside him or her. I experienced this. When you are flying, there's only one thought: now the plane took the necessary direction, now the pilot dropped the speed... The door opens; you'll have to go now... And during the jumps, you think not about yourself, but about the best way to jump; you follow the airport, the target, the way your body falls, and the wind. There's no time for fear.

Once though I was really scared. The wind suddenly picked up and moved me close to a herd of cattle. I thought that I might land right on their horns, and this thought scared me. But when the first fright left me, I calmed down and started to move the ropes. I landed successfully, quickly put the parachute down and looked at the cattle with these huge horns.

Our group jumped a lot. From the simple jumps we passed to some more complicated ones. We learned to land into the very center of the cross. We jumped from different heights, different locations of the plane, to the ground and into the water, during strong frosts and calm warm days, in the night and in the sunrise. Our instructor taught us to be patient in the air and to develop will power.

As time passed, my family got used to my hobby. And still every time I went to the airport they were worrying, especially when I returned later than usual. "So, how did you land today?" asked mom nervously. And I told her about my adventures.

The airport of our club was located not far from our house. It could be easily seen from the window of mom's room. The place was called Karachikha. Maybe this was not a perfect sounding word, but for us it sounded great. We all were in love with Karachikha. We even sang about it all together when returning home:

> Karachikha.
> Oh, Karachikha, my.
> It is a rough road that leads to the sky.
> To my quiet and unknown distant star,
> O'er the threshold we step from where we are.

Karachikha became our second home. We ran there in the morning, if we worked the evening shift, and at nights, sometimes during the cold winter days, sometimes in the rainy fall.

Waiting for their turn to jump, our guys created another funny song:

> A passerby notices my chute in early morn,
>
> And with slight reproach shakes his head in concern.
>
> "Just who in the devil blew you under the cloud?"
>
> But he wishes us anyway "The Best Luck" out loud.

There were many girls in the club. But perhaps, the most successful parachutist was my friend Tanya Torchilova. She was very fragile, feminine, and she liked art very much. Tanya studied in the art college. She jumped bravely and precisely. She always landed and caught the parachute a few meters from the circle center. After every such jump Tanya had such a big smile on her face, as if it was her birthday.

Honestly, not everything was perfect in my performance. I would jump successfully a couple of times, and then suddenly have failures, landing too far away from the landing circle every time. And again, a kind person helped me.

He was a former military pilot named Pavel Mihajlovich Tapersky. This person, who was not young, a colonel in the reserves, was in love with his profession. Pavel Mihajlovich gave many years of his life to the military service, but after his retirement, in spite of his weakening health, he tried to keep up with us young people. And not only could he keep up with us, he was even giving us energy. We could only envy his will and love for the sky. He saw distinctly the goal and tended to it constantly. It was Pavel Mihajlovich who helped me by his own example and kind advice.

Later we started jumps with extension, where we would wait a long time to open the parachute. I waited for this day so impatiently, and it went so badly that I don't even want to remember it. It was the first time I felt so helpless in the air. I twisted as if I didn't know parachute-jumping theory at all. When I landed, I almost cried. Was it I who thought that I could handle a perfect jump? We were preparing for the regional competition at that time.

The YaK-12, like a big dragonfly, slowly rose into the air. The right door of the cabin is removed and the cold jets of air get through it and cool down my warm face. Near me, with a hand on the control handle, sits a person with an important title: instructor pilot-parachutist. I envy his calmness and patience, but still I can't get ready for the jump.

For about the fiftieth time, to the command "Go!" I leave the plane and rush down, into the embrace of my native Yaroslavl down below. For some reason, I didn't show great success in a free fall in combination with an extended jump. Sometimes it was ok, sometimes not. And for participating in these competitions, one must show stable results. How I wanted to jump perfectly this time! "Ready?" asks the instructor quietly. The height is eight hundred meters. Under the plane's wing I see the line of the railways, after it, the green field of the airport with the famous cross in the white circle. "Go!" Strongly, maybe even too strongly, I push from the plane, and feel immediately that the jump didn't come out well. With difficulty I stop twisting, there's no more thought about the "beauty of style," the only concern is not to fall into a spin.

I land so-so, terribly upset with myself. Our instructor Valentin Ivanovich Diukov, after watching my falling, adds several fair but ironic commentaries about my "style." What should I do? I went away from the group, sat down to analyze my failure, almost ready to cry. I'll never become a true parachutist! They teach me everything, and I still can't learn. Ok, I won't ever jump again!

Here was my friend Tanya Torchilova running to me. One look at me was enough for her to understand everything. She scolded me for my weakness and practically pulled me to the start. We still had to compete in precision landing.

While the plane gained height, I calmed down completely and pulled myself together. I jumped well, landed several meters away from the circle. Valentin Ivanovich Diukov was the first to warmly congratulate me.

It's harder to dive in a group. When you jump alone, you don't feel so upset when you miss the target. This is the failure of your own self. On the contrary, when you show bad results in a group jump, the whole team fails. That's why you're trying to do your best, holding on even when you feel that there is no more strength left. If you can't hold both ropes, you hold only one, and still slowly, centimeter by centimeter, approach the center of the target.

A MAN IN SPACE!

It was a wonderful morning on April 12, 1961. The usual sounds of a working city came through the open window; a cool wind brought the smell of early spring.

Suddenly there was a sound of quick steps, then again. The door opened and somebody shouted in a voice trembling with excitement, "Hooray! It's happened! It's finally happened! Hooray to Gagarin!" Still not having a clue of what had happened, I darted out of the office and ran to the office of the Communist Committee secretary. The office was already crowded. Everybody gathered near the old radio. Someone was rapidly turning the handle and still couldn't find a proper radio channel.

And suddenly it was, "And now news from TASS, about the first ever flight of a man into the cosmic space..." The voice of the announcer sounded unusually solemn. People were listening to it without breathing, afraid to miss a word. Our eyes were sparkling with the pride for our country and its dear son, Yury Alekseevich Gagarin.

The announcer stopped talking. Then we heard solemn music from the speaker. And then I can't remember without a smile what started in the office after the news program. Everyone in the room suddenly started to talk, shout and laugh. Nobody listened to anyone, and this was not necessary. One thing was clear; the unique flight of Gagarin gave everlasting glory to our Motherland, our people. This was so wonderful; joy and happiness filled our souls, tears unwillingly came to the eyes.

GOODBYE, YAROSLAVL!

"Space exploration"—this phrase came into our life, and turned everything around it. Half a year ago we first heard about the flight of Yury Gagarin. Soon after German Titov made almost eighteen circles around the Earth. It started to happen. Maybe soon a Soviet woman would climb into space, and say loudly for everyone to hear, "Hello universe!"

We girls tried to imagine the first woman cosmonaut. We imagined her our own way; the guys didn't agree with us and drew different pictures of her. There were many arguments. We never reached agreement, though we all knew that this first woman cosmonaut would start from a Soviet airport.

For me this arguing had a special, "hidden" sense. On April 12, 1961, I developed a disease called "space." I don't know how the doctors classify this disease and what they prescribe to curc it, but it seems to me that this disease does exist.

On the day of Gagarin's flight, not yet being able to get through the chaos of my own feelings, I already started to feel some nervousness, some shy thoughts. Everything fell into place only when I read in a newspaper that Gagarin was a student of an aerospace club, just like I was. And then I decided. I'll be an cosmonaut.

Of course I realized that these were the feelings of millions and millions of Soviet people in those days. Perhaps thousands of them wrote requests to admit them into the team of cosmonauts. The "competition" was outrageous. One had to compete with many strong candidates. But still...

Nobody knew about this except Valentina Fyodorovna Ousova. "I have just one question for you," I asked her after entering her office. "But this is the question of life and death. Valentina Fyodorovna, tell me the truth. Will they accept me if I write a request?"

Ousova didn't hurry with the answer. I stood silently, trying to hide the nervousness and stop shaking.

"Well, Valyusha," she said finally, "If you feel you're ready for this, write the application to the school of cosmonauts. I trust you. I know you won't fail us."

The letter was signed. That is why the term "spaceflights" had this special sense for me.

In December of 1961 I was called to the regional committee of the National Association Supporting of Aviation and Fleet. It's difficult to give all of the details of the conversation with a colonel of Military Air Forces. I thought it was unreal. I was afraid to even think of my luck, not to scare it away. I understood only one thing; they invited me to start training for the flight in a spaceship. We all believed in the reality of this flight then, but no one thought that it might happen so soon.

Spring came slowly. Nights were still frosty, but in the daytime the sky was deep blue, and the Sun was shining and there was snow melting.

Challenging and interesting work was waiting for me, and I still couldn't get used to the thought that I was leaving Yaroslavl, saying goodbye to the city and places so dear to my heart, wandering along its silent streets at night.

Farewell, Yaroslavl! Farewell, Volga! Farewell, Karachikha! See you again! If it were possible, I would leave my heart to the people of this city. My thanks to them! Thank you, Valentina Fyodorovna. Thank you, uncle Vasya, our teacher. Thank you, Ljudmila Alekseevna Kosmoleva, Tosya Vinogradova, Aleksey Georgiyevich Agafonov, Valentin Ivanovitch Dyunov, Kondratyev, Morozytchev, my dear friends and comrades.

IN THE FAMILY OF STAR BROTHERS

Let me tell you, when I entered the "Star City" of cosmonauts, my heart was about to stop. How will they meet me there? I didn't do anything great in my life; in fact, I didn't see much of a real life and these were real pilots and two of them, Gagarin and Titov, were heroes whose names were known all over the world.

And what about us girls? Well, we jumped with parachutes, new small planes. That's all we did. But I tried to be calm.

The hall we entered was quite empty. We looked around. The walls were covered with the pictures of cosmonauts training, class schedules, schemes, and graphs. How complicated they seemed to us at that time!

Our nervousness calmed down after a while. We even turned on the television in the corner of the room and started to watch some program. And then the guys came. They came in a big group, all neatly dressed. All of them were officers. We felt a little awkward but this lasted for only a minute because one of the guys approached and simply said, "Let's be friends, girls. My name is…" And he told us his name. It was German Titov. Then the rest introduced themselves, too. We were shaking their strong hands, called out our names, answered their questions, and laughed at their jokes.

At this time I can't recall many details of the day we all met. But this is not so important. What was important is that the men accepted us. At this moment our friendship started. It helped us later when the lessons and the training started.

Within two or three days we knew all our colleagues. Yury Gagarin, German Titov, Andriyan Nikolayev, Pavel Popvitch, my future space partner Valery Bykovsky, the future cosmonauts Number 7, 8, 9, and 12 became our best friends.

Later I vas thinking many times about this first meeting, asking myself: what impression did they make on me, those who were ready to fly to the stars? Modesty. Perhaps this was the feature of everyone. They also were united by openness and their passion for their work, their profession. This passion gave them strength and helped to overcome hardships and barriers. And there were lots of challenges. Among them was a question: can a woman fly to space?

Since long ago there has been a belief that a woman was a weak creature. There is even an expression "the weaker sex." Is it really fair? By going through training, we as people needed to answer this question. The opinion of the scientists and doctors was quite different. Some believe that in certain ways a female body is stronger and more able to survive than a male one. Others were convinced of the opposite. There were questions of how to organize our training, what criteria to use in its evaluation, how big should be the load, the exercises, and all the rest?

Naturally, the g-forces to which all pilots become accustomed were too big for us. At the same time the pressure that exists while moving toward the orbit and while descending in the spaceship required similar preparation from us. But pressure is not the only factor that gives special requirements for the cosmonaut's body. Some specialists in "space medicine" say that during the long period of weightlessness, one may experience the muscles weakening and other organs slowing down. To shield a cosmonaut from such problems, he or she should develop the necessary physical strength before the flight.

Many such concerns were simplified in training men. All of them were excellent sportsmen. Weights, gymnastics, athletics, skiing, swimming, and other sport games were something they were used to. After running ninety minutes on the football field, they felt quite energetic and able to work. Pull-ups, push-ups, and more than 30 seconds of hanging with the legs held at an angle to the body; none of these exercises were serious for them.

A military pilot becomes accustomed to courage by his profession. A shy and weak person should not fly. But what about us? We girls were not cowards. Nobody could accuse us of being weak, either. But still much had to be done to prepare us for space flight.

First of all, we were introduced to a range of technologies, training, and devices that we had to learn on our long and difficult way to space. Our flight, as Yury Gagarin fairly remarked once, started on the ground. We went from lab to lab. One of them had a "treadmill," a wide, moving path. Try to stand on it, and it will rush with a high speed under your feet. You have to run not to be thrown back. The speed is controlled by the doctors from the control console. Many measurement devices were put on the running person to monitor the frequency of breathing, pulse, and the heart work.

We had to learn every device, gadget etc. The flight stimulator left such an impression. The cabin was moving in three dimensions. The chair with a person was rotating across one axis, the frame where the cabin was fixed in the second one, and the whole construction in the third. It all looked like a complex carousel. Our heads were spinning just watching it.

Group Two: Above: Early Soviet cosmonauts: left to right (first row): Anikeev, Yorkina, Popovich, Tereshkova, Solovyova; (second raw): Shonin, Belyaev, Titov, Nikolaev, Nelyubov, Khrunov, Komarov, Gagarin, Volynov, Gorbatko, Leonov

Seeing our hesitation, doctors and engineers who conducted the training turned on the two-way radio. Now for the questions they were asking they would get one same answer from the cabin: feels ok, the health state is normal. They explained to us, cosmonaut can meet similar conditions during the flight, so he or she should be well prepared."

We saw the heat chamber, where a person has to fulfill a whole set of complicated tasks, and then the centrifuge. And finally, we say an isolation chamber, a special chamber that was absolutely isolated from the outside world and didn't transfer a single sound. Inside of it the future cosmonauts had to spend many days begin quite alone. In this "cabin of silence" German Titov was reading loud the poems of Pushkin, Pavel Popovitch sang Ukrainian songs, and Valery Bykovsky drew cartoons.

Lessons started at once, without any preparation. Along with the others, I attended the lectures, studied the techniques unfamiliar to me before, got physical training and worked out.

From the start, the guys from the group of cosmonauts treated me with care and supervision having their rights as the "elders." And when they thought that enough time had passed for my inclusion into the rhythm of the "Star City," they started to show their irritation with my shy steps on the unknown ground. During classes I often sat near Gagarin or Titov. We were right next to each other, like school kids, at the same desk. I had to do everything they did: work with a key; take the signals; decipher them; and make astronomers' tables. It was so hard to compete with them! Sometimes I would lose every hope but the guys were encouraging me, on!"

As time passed, I got accustomed to the new conditions of my life and work. The works of Tsiolkovsky, Tsander, and Meschersky became interesting and understandable for me. And the men started to treat me as an equal; they agreed or argued with me, shared their successes and sorrows, asked me questions, and telling me about their plans. In general, they accepted me into their "cosmic family" without even a shadow of coldness or special accommodation to the "weaker sex."

With time I got used to the phrase, "Come on, don't be shy, do it like a man would," as our instructors would tell us. From the very beginning my girlfriend and I took it suspiciously, but then we realized that everything is done here without any excuses to the "weak gender." Of course, some corrections were made to us girls, taking into account our abilities. But these corrections were very slight.

From the very start, my girlfriend and I loved living in the "Star City." We didn't even notice how the team of cosmonauts became our second home, second family. It's easy to remember it now. But at that time... Of course, my heart of a common factory girl was beating with happiness. I am in a family of those who conquer space! I thought about it with a sense of special pride. And most importantly, all the people, heroes and those not known as heroes, were close, friendly, and so approachable. They never let my friend and me out of their attention, noticing even a slightest change in our mood. They were interested in our well-being, news from our families, invited us to their family parties, and didn't forget to wish us happy birthday.

I soon got an apartment outside the training facility. It was bright and cozy. I was happy about it! I was consumed by choosing and arranging furniture, imagining how I would invite my new friends for a house-warming. I very often happened to be a guest of the families of Gagarin,

Popovitch, Bykovsky, and also of our instructors and doctors. At that time I wanted to be in the role of hostess myself.

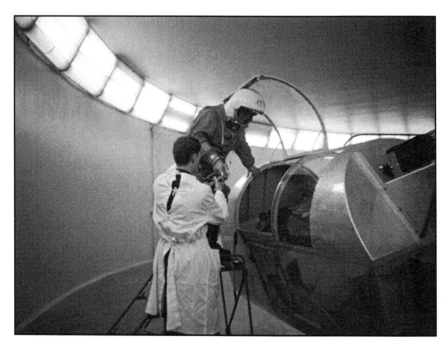

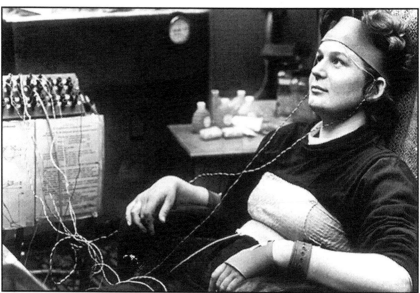

STEPS TO THE COSMODROME

Several times during the training I visited the place where the magic ships were built and met those who constructed them and turned the dreams to life. This was a big group of wonderful people who gave all their knowledge and power, all their talents and work of the mind to the development of our spaceflights. We were told about the birth of each ship, and were shown the processes of its creation.

With great appreciation, I kept the present from the Chief Designer (Sergei Korolev), the small "Lunik," the copy of our banner brought to the Moon. The conversation with this great person will remain in my heart all my life. Every word he said resonated in my heart. How I wanted to hurry up the time of my spaceflight so I could look into the eyes of these people with the sense of fulfillment and self-confidence. Even at that time I was already searching for the kind words to thank them for their work and care.

Days flew by. They sped up into weeks and months filled with training and studies in the "Star City," and at the same time common works and studies went on in the "Starry Town." These were the steps towards the launch site or cosmodrome. Those were hard, very hard steps.

We studied and trained frequently, picked up different sports that helped us to develop the balance, smoothen our moves, and train the eyesight. I was fond of skiing, skating, boating, swimming and diving. I did not mind riding a bike, but for a long time I was afraid of jumping on the "battuta," a hanging net or trampoline.

It does not look hard, to jump from the net or fall on it and make a forward or backward flip. The figures of "higher pilot skills" come out more slowly, but very effectively. It's not by chance that in a circus the acrobats who jump on such nets always have a great success.

But it only looks easy when well-trained sportsmen do such exercises. Not all people find it easy to learn such "easy" jumps. I belonged to this group of people. It was easier for me to jump into the river Kotorosl from the 12-meter bridge, than to make a half turn over the "battuta." My co-student joked that I had a "face in squares." This was because, sometimes instead of making a turn in the air, I would suddenly "stick" to the net with my forehead and thus get a memento for being so slow.

I still remember one of the last exercises I did on the trampoline in Yaroslavl. It happened that on that day my jumps were extremely successful. I did more and more turns over the net, one after another. "Go," yelled the guys. Again I flew up and then...fell on my head. A sharp ache. The diagnosis by the "specialists": I had twisted my neck. After this accident I couldn't turn my head for several days.

Yet I did learn to control my body in the air, in spite of the pessimistic forecasts of the instructors. As it's said, it's not only the net that a parachutist knows.

It's hard to give a step-by-step description of my training in the "Star City." Our program included lessons in flying planes. The pilots gave me one more "ticket to the sky." I had to not only study the plane with its complex equipment, but to take its wheel and learn to fly this machine with wings.

Many times we would rise to the sky with my instructor, a kind and patient teacher, a great master of his profession. Our early flights must have been boring to this professional pilot-instructor but he was insistent and very patient. Not everything went smoothly; there were failures that brought me to despair, but he kept his cool. Others might have yelled at me, but not him. "One more time," I heard his calm and encouraging voice, and we repeated it all from the very beginning, element by element.

I would return home tired, but happy with each new day that brought me closer to the magic point. I often thought: why do I not succeed in everything? I asked my instructor, and got the answer that brought more confidence in me. "Don't be embarrassed, Valya," he tried to persuade me, "You are trying to accomplish a science which is new for you, the science of being a pilot, and it is not as simple as it may look from the ground."

My instructors taught me many details of this extremely complicated science, corrected me when I was mistaken, and taught, taught, and taught it all over again.

I saw the Baikonur Cosmodrome with its launch pad and a giant rocket for the first time on the day of the flight of Andriyan Nikolayev and Pavel Popovitch. A beautiful sight opened in front of my eyes, a sight I could only imagine based on the stories of my friends and instructors. At that time I knew I was getting closer to my own launch.

The first two-person space trip had lasted for several days; it not only gave new information to the scientists and the constructors, but also brought some changes into our training program.

The training became more intense. The improved equipment brought greater demands. Every new flight meant new achievements, new experience. All of it allowed us to reevaluate the past and to select the best approaches. We had to not only pass all sets of training requirements, but to allow doctors, scientists, and engineers to conduct new experiments during and after the flight.

Not long after that flight, four candidates were selected from the whole group. This group was called "the group ready for the flight." It included Valery Bykovsky with his alternate partner, my (female) friend (Irena Solovyeva) and me. At first no one among us knew who would be the first to get into the cabin of a spaceship. But as for the training, we all, one in his/her turn, got into the learner's cabin that was located in one of the rooms of our building. We all participated in the conduct of each "flight" and waited impatiently for our "Star Hour."

ONE HUNDRED SIXTY TWO PLUS ONE

In a couple of minutes I jump. As always, I worry a little, try to concentrate. There is no fear. I'm absolutely sure in the success of the task that I'm going to accomplish. It is sort of like the feeling of a sportsman that staying still just before pushing off. Maybe this is the feeling of a soldier ready to stand up and attack to win.

This jump will not be the same as the previous one hundred sixty two sky dives. I won't hear the familiar command "Go!" I won't jump with my head forward through the open door of a plane, won't fall with my hands stretched in the air toward the Earth so dear to my heart. Everything will be different. Totally different...

The launch pad of the cosmodrome. Steady, beautiful rocket, sparkling with silver, points its cone to the zenith. It is correctly the miracle of the 20th century. It is ready to carry the spaceship *Vostok 6* to the stars, the spaceship I have the honor to command.

Am I ready for a spaceflight? I believe I am. I remember many months of training; the load was impressive, just the same that male cosmonauts had, without any discounts. There are no "female" spaceships with more comfortable flight conditions.

My launch... Only yesterday we accompanied Valery Bykovsky to his launch. He's a cheerful and nice guy, our Valero. I remember how he joked once. If a girl flies to space, he would attach a little pocket for lipstick and other cosmetics near the mirror fixed on the right sleeve of the cosmonaut's dress. We were laughing then and thanking him for his idea, telling him that we would sure do that when the time comes, and here it came.

A familiar voice appears in the speakers from time to time. This is Valery. His signal, "Yastreb," is already known to the whole world. During the connection times I was in the mission control center, I saw Valery on the control monitors, and shouted, forgetting where I was, "I see you Valera. We see you. Do you hear? Smile if you do. We got flowers for you!" "Do I deserve them?" the space would answer with a familiar voice, and the face of Valery had a hardly noticeable smile.

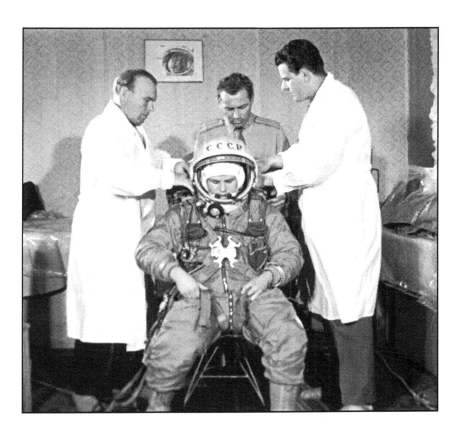

"Yastreb, Yastreb, do you recognize me?" asked I, "Greetings to you, our warmest greetings!" There was a short phrase from the space, "I'm waiting!"

It seems that we were together just yesterday, just now, but there are already two days that separate our launches. Before the flight Valery sat on the bench in the garden and looked up thinking about something. And there was the sky, where the hot winds blew across it, seldom washed with rains, surprisingly blue sky, clear and so high. Valery was so right when he said, "A person doesn't stay alone in space. There are also those who created this machine, who prepared it for the flight there on the ground. Those, who are watching you, doctors, and our friends, they are all near, they are flying into space, too."

The last days before the launch, my backup and I once again felt the friendly care and touching attention of our men. They didn't leave us alone. With cheerful jokes or seriously, they gave us the last instructions, helped with advice, took us fishing and cooked a great fish soup over an open fire. They entertained us as they could.

Andriyan was especially attentive to us. He offered his help, advised us to rest more, to not think about anything, and "not to lose our calm no matter what happens."

When there were still one or two days left, I was calm. But I got nervous right before the start. I can't even tell why. Yury Gagarin noticed it, but instead of saying something that would make me calm, he sympathized with me, "I understand you. It's hard to be the first."

The arrow slowly moves across the watch. It seems to me that a long, long time ago I was left alone with my thoughts inside a sealed spaceship. But no, I still feel the warmth of the friendly hands, hugs of those who followed me; there is still the nice smell of the grass and flowers in the cabin. Here are the voices of my friends that became familiar now to millions of people. My friends, cosmonauts, exploring the universe for humanity, sent the warm greetings from the orbits to all peoples of the Earth.

I am on the launch pad. "Chaika, Chaika," calls Berkut with the voice of

Yury Gagarin. He asks if I feel ok. I answer that I do feel well, and it is true. I am not nervous any longer; there is just the expectation of something unknown and wonderful ahead.

But there's no more time for thoughts. The arrow of the watch erases my last minutes on Earth. The Chief Designer speaks to me, then Yury again. I feel that they are trying to distract me, encourage me, for a successful flight. Kind, dear people! How thankful I am for your sympathy and work!

A minute to launch readiness is announced. Knock, knock, knock. The metronome counts seconds. No, this is not a metronome. This is my heart.

The last words and wishes...

Twelve hours and thirty minutes Moscow time... Start! The music of launch begins with the low sounds. I hear the roar that reminds me of the sound of thunder. The rocket is shaking like a thin tree under the wind. The roar grows, becomes wider, more upper notes are distinguished in it. The spaceship is shivering.

Unexpectedly, I say to myself, "I'm flying." This was prompted as I feel my heavy hands and feet, the hidden weights that were shaking my chest. The weight grows. It becomes hard to breathe; I can't move a single finger. The guys told me that's how it's going to be. So, everything is ok then!

Somewhere in the star-filled height flies the lonely spaceship controlled by Valery Bykovsky, Valerka, as all guys call him friendly. "I'm waiting," he said to me during his recent talk with the Earth, and then he smiles from the television screen. And here's *Vostok 6* approaching the point of meeting for the two Soviet spaceships on the orbit of Earth.

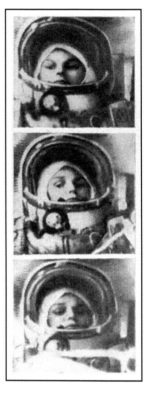

The titanic force of the boiling gases tears away the Earth's gravitation. I feel like the weight reached its limit, but it still grows. How much time passed since the start? A minute? An hour? A day? I cannot collect my thoughts; I know I have to, but cannot.

"Chaika, Chaika, everything is excellent, the machine is working great." I shake with surprise. The voice of Yury Gagarin sounds right near, as if he's sitting next to me, as an instructor in the right seat of the plane. I answer not at once; maybe, because of the cheering words of my friend, maybe, the flight to the orbit is over, and the pressure disappeared, as it melted under the warm wave spreading in my body. Breathing became easy.

I open my eyes and look out of the illuminator. (Illuminator is the porthole.) In a loud voice, I comment about what I see, "I am Chaika. I see the horizon. There is a blue stripe. This is the Earth. How beautiful it is! Everything is going well."

Hello universe!

"RENDEZVOUS" IN SPACE

I believe that time will come when people will fly to space to relax, for a chance to distract themselves from the everyday Earth routine. Doctors state that even a short change in scenery makes a person fresh, restores the spirits.

Right now a spaceship has little in common with a cozy room in some resort. However, if you turn the radio off, you can enjoy the complete silence.

On Earth we get frustrated when our neighbor turns the radio up loud and thus interrupts our leisure. In space you will hardly be able to sleep if the radio is off. It remains the only thread that connects us to all that is so close and dear to our hearts. This can be a warm word of your friend, and a favorite tune, and some important advice. Space flight is work, and unusual work.

It seems that a human has nothing to do inside the spaceship when flying to orbit in such a perfect apparatus as "Vostok." You could give the analogy of a plane flying by autopilot. Flying a plane may even seem more complicated; the equipment should control its location, make corrections to the course and the height of the flight, avoid the stormy clouds, and watch carefully the changes of the air conditions.

Spaceflight is not at all like this! Just relax in a chair, eat something delicious, drink water, and watch the wonderful halo of the Earth. The automatic systems will do everything for you; they will lead you to the orbit and return to the Earth. It will warm you and bring you to sleep, and almost wish you goodnight.

Of course, it doesn't work like this. The work day of a cosmonaut is very busy. All the experiments, observations, trials, radio connections, and other activities leave almost no free time. Add to this the serious psychological load; the space flight at several hundreds kilometers from the native planet is not yet a typical occupation for a person.

The main thing is that a human is not a guest on a spaceship, but its master, a commander. You should be ready to meet any unexpected event during a flight in an unknown environment, should be able, if necessary, to take over the control of the ship and fly it to the place of landing. It's not by chance that all my "star brothers" are former military pilots. And it's not in vain that my insistent and patient instructors spent so much time to teach me and my female friends to fly the plane. There is a fair saying that aviation is the cradle of spaceflights.

On the orbit, I call Valery, "Yastreb, Yastreb, I'm Chaika. Do you hear me ok?" Yastreb replies immediately. His voice is cheerful, full of energy, as if someone else, not he, has been wandering in the sixth ocean for three days. Bravo, Valerka!

I'm trying to get used to the absence of gravity. I can't do it at once; it's too unusual for me. It is unusual, but not frightening, maybe rather pleasant. In fact, for a long time before the flight of a human into space, some western scientists predicted death for those people who would stay without gravity for a long time. Andriyan Nikolayev and Pavel Popovitch proved it was not so.

I'm watching through the illuminator our beautiful planet, its halo discovered by the first traveler to the stars, Yury Alekseevich Gagarin. I shut the illuminator when the blinding Sun's rays shine into it. When the ship flies over the dark half of the Earth, I train in defining the constellations that are as bright and shiny as the cleaned buttons on a military uniform. The radio connection is kept on all the time.

Imperceptibly, I got accustomed to the lack of gravity and remembered it only when I was going to do something "Earth-like." Thus during the first "night" (this term is very relative for a cosmonaut because his or her "day" equals to the time of one turn around the Earth) I woke up because of a very strong and unusual feeling. I didn't understand at once where I was and what was happening to me. It happened that I was awakened by my own "floating" hands.

I remembered the advice of the "space veterans"—German Titov, Pavel Popovitch, and Andriyan Nikolayev—placed my hands under the belts of the fixing system, and went to sleep immediately.

On June 17, 3 pm Moscow time, I flew over my native Yaroslavl, over the Volga. I was looking to the Earth, all in white clouds, so hard that my eyes were aching, and it seemed to me that I saw a thin silver stripe, a familiar contour of the ancient city. Maybe, I just wanted this so badly. I passed on a hello to my mom and to all mothers in the world; asked mom not to worry; everything was going well.

On the 19th of June the flight program was entirely completed. However sad it was to part with the tamed space, the soul was anxious to fly back to our native planet, to the friends and close people. I want everything to be in its place, the clouds to flow over the head, not under the feet, the wind to make noise in the leaves of the trees, the Sun to hide in the horizon, covered with the purple hue.

The honor of landing first belonged to Valery. But he, like a gentleman, gave me the first turn, and wished me a smooth finish. During the 49th orbit, the roar of the brake engines struck my ears, which had become used to the silence of space. *Vostok 6* left orbit and descended toward the Earth.

...Again the pressure pushes me in the chair, shuts my eyes. I notice the dark red tongues of the flame outside the windows. I'm trying to memorize, fix all the feelings, all peculiarities of this descending, to tell those, who will be conquering space after me. My mind is working calmly and logically. Our equipment won't fail; the ship will land exactly at the destination point.

With a loud roar, the spaceship bumps into the dense atmosphere. The noise grows with every second; it already reminds me of the thunder of hundreds of drums, the part of some outrageous heroic symphony, glorifying a citizen of the Earth, its grandeur and glory that reached space in our days.

Hello, my dear Russia!

* * *

Photos of Valentina Tereshkova, prior to joining the cosmonaut program.

Valentina Tereshkova, left, at parachuting school.

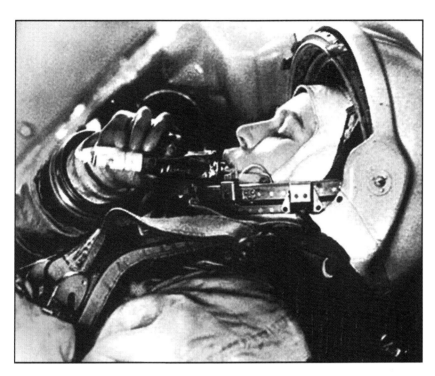

Vostok 6 photos.

On 3 November 1963, Valentina Tereshkova married fellow cosmonaut, Andriyan Grigoryevich Nikolayev. They had one daughter, Elena Andriyanovna.

Valentina Tereshkova with Yuri Gagarin.

Valentina Tereshkova with Neil Armstrong, 1970.

Valentina Tereshkova with Yuri Gagarin.

Valentina Tereshkova (*Vostok 6*) with Valery Bykovsky (*Vostok 5*) at a promotional event for children.

Enjoy Reading Space History?

Then you should sign up to receive the magazine, *Quest: The History of Spaceflight*.

Published since 1992, *Quest* is the only peer-reviewed journal focused on the history of space. Each 64-page quarterly issue features interviews, research papers, and the stories of the space age—from human spaceflight to military space, from robotic exploration to policy and politics, from the efforts of individuals to the efforts of international government. Get the inside stories...and the stories behind the stories!

It's time to join with the thousands of people who've read *Quest*.

THE HISTORY OF SPACEFLIGHT
Q U A R T E R L Y

Preserving the history of spaceflight...

One story at a time

Visit www.spacehistory101.com and sign up today!

23354046R00033

Printed in Great Britain
by Amazon